FREEING
RADICAL HERO

**FIGHTING THE
IMPOSTOR MINDSET**

LOU SOLOMON

**Freeing Your Radical Hero:
Fighting the Impostor Mindset**
By Lou M. Solomon

Published by Interact Skills LLC
1435 West Morehead Street, Studio 210, Charlotte, NC 28208

Copyright © 2017 by Interact Skills LLC. All rights reserved. This book, or parts thereof, may not be reproduced in any form without permission. The scanning, uploading and distribution of this book via the Internet without the permission of the publisher is prohibited. Your support of the author's rights is appreciated.

This is a book of non-fiction; however, some of the names and characteristics of individuals involved have been changed to protect their privacy.

Design and production by SPARK Publications
SPARKpublications.com

Printing History: Edition One, June 2017, ISBN 978-1-943070-24-4

Library of Congress Control Number: 2017943994

PSY031000 PSYCHOLOGY / Social Psychology
SEL040000 SELF-HELP / Communication & Social Skills
SEL027000 SELF-HELP / Personal Growth / Success

Printed in the United States of America

To the Radical Hero in you

TABLE OF CONTENTS

SECTION I: THE PROBLEM

There's a Name for That **9**
So What Causes Impostor Syndrome? **13**
The Trigger Called Public Speaking............................ **16**
Not You? **18**
The Perfectionism Come-On **22**

SECTION II: FREEING THE RADICAL HERO

Miracle Readiness **27**
Confronting the Self-Talk **29**
Your Radical Hero **31**

SECTION III: LIES AND LIMITING BELIEFS

LIMITING BELIEF #1
   Control Is Power; Vulnerability Is Weakness **47**
LIMITING BELIEF #2
   There's Nothing Original or Gifted about Me **64**
LIMITING BELIEF #3
   A Successful Career Is a Successful Life **70**

LIMITING BELIEF #4
I Don't Have a Real Story.. **85**
LIMITING BELIEF #5
Loud Talkers Are in Charge..................................... **135**
The Way It Is Today.. **150**

SUPPLEMENT 154

RESOURCES 158

Acknowledgments: A Grateful Heart **162**

About the Author **163**

FOREWORD

My life has always made more sense in the rearview mirror. I see how all the dots connect; I understand how the rough spots have been a gift. I'm guessing it's that way for you too.

Today I can trace the trek I've made to get here. I know how my life has prepared me to help people find their voices through authentic speaking.

A while back I began working on a book entitled *Real Influence*. For months I wrote and wrote and wrote. But I was writing around something. Driving home one day I thought, "*What* is keeping me from writing this story?" I heard a whisper: "The first story. You have to tell the first story." With that, my grip on the wheel loosened a bit. "Of course," I thought, "that's it."

What lay ahead was more than I expected. I knew I would have to be vulnerable on a whole new level if I wanted to share what I've learned about fighting the impostor mindset. What I didn't expect was the gift of more space—more freedom.

In the fall of 2016, I gave a TEDx Talk called "The Surprising Solution to the Impostor Syndrome," which was the inspiration for this book. Moved by the people who reached out to me, I wrote this book in the few months that followed.

Freeing Your Radical Hero: Fighting the Impostor Mindset is a little book of honesty, answers, and exercises to help you call out impostor thinking at whatever level it occurs for you. My hope is that you'll find it simple, down to earth, and explorer-friendly.

I'm going to make a safe assumption that if you're reading this, you're in the club. Welcome. You're in great company. I've watched droves of smart, successful, lovable people come through my studio and share that they've struggled with public speaking because it triggers impostor thinking. For many of these super-achievers, the impostor experience goes beyond the times they're asked to speak publicly. They live with the feeling that they haven't earned their success.

However and whenever impostor thinking shows up for you, hear this—you are stronger than you know. You were meant for something much greater.

Lou Solomon

Summer 2017

SECTION I

THE PROBLEM

There's a Name for That

Years ago, I was sitting across from Barbara in her office. Barbara was a wonderful human being and a brilliant therapist. She also had a great sense of humor. I adored her. I was telling her about my career when she said, "Lou, you've been successful haven't you? You've had some big jobs. Do you see yourself as successful?"

I said, "Well, I've been pretty lucky. I've managed to be at the right place at the right time."

Barbara eyed me for a moment and said, "There's a name for the way you always push back on the idea that you had anything to do with your success. It's called the impostor syndrome."

Have you ever heard something that ran up your backbone and made the world slow to a crawl? Barbara was giving a name to the internal struggle I had known since I was a kid. As she continued, I felt a window opening in my heart and mind.

She explained that the impostor syndrome is the inability of successful people to internalize their success. They write off their accomplishments as luck. They believe they've somehow fooled others into thinking they're more talented than they really are.

That day I became a self-researcher, from the inside out. It has been crucial for me to understand the nature of "impostor thinking" and to put this experience into words to bring value to others.

An estimated 70 percent of successful people in this country experience symptoms and feelings associated with impostor syndrome at some point in their lives. I like to call those symptoms the fantastic four: anxiety, perfectionism, self-doubt, and fear of failure.

Seventy percent seems low. That means that only two out of every three people in this world ever experience feelings of self-doubt, for example. I'm guessing that almost all of us know a thing or two about the fantastic four.

Even the great Maya Angelo said that each time she published a book she wondered if this would be the time people would discover that she had been running a game on them. With all the evidence of her amazing talent, Maya Angelo wondered if people would discover her as a fraud.

THE FORMAL RESEARCH

Whether used in combination with "syndrome," "mindset," "phenomenon," or "thinking," the word "impostor" has reverberated through study after study that supports the original work of Pauline Clance and Suzanne Imes in 1974.

In a study of high-achieving women, Clance and Imes found the majority were unable to internalize their success, despite undeniable evidence of their talent.

A key characteristic of the high achievers studied by Clance and Imes (along with the scores of researchers since) was the fear that people would see them as not having earned their success.

The severity of impostor thinking has been measured in both men and women by their level of identification with statements such as:

"I feel I don't deserve
the recognition I receive."

"People tend to believe I'm more
talented than I really am."

"I consider my accomplishments
inadequate for my stage in life."

"I dwell on incidents in which I didn't do my
best more than those times I did do my best."

"When taking on new projects,
I worry I'm not qualified."

Since new jobs, big transitions, and public speaking can trigger impostor thinking, an individual might score low on the scale at one point in life and moderate or high at another.

So What Causes Impostor Syndrome?

Typically, impostor feelings are rooted in the family. When parents focus on being smart and successful over inner self-worth, for example, kids can confuse their worth as tied only to achievement.

In my case, I grew up with constant criticism. My father was a decorated pilot. People admired him in the outside world. But at home he was a raging alcoholic and an abuser who berated everyone for being incompetent. My response to his belittling was to swear an oath to the behavior that would protect me from the humiliation of incompetence. I worked at being the perfect child—quiet, well behaved, neat, and smart.

But even when I brought home straight As, my father speculated that the school I was attending was too easy. And like most kids, I believed the only true feedback I was hearing was at home. I saw myself as fooling the people on the outside with achievements that weren't real.

Now, an unhappy childhood is not a pre-requisite to impostor thinking. Impostor thinking also shows up in individuals who are the first in the family to make it out of the neighborhood or earn a college degree; people who have attained success very early in their careers and worry that it's not real; and people in creative fields, such as actors, musicians and artists.

Susan, an extraordinary artist and a good friend, once told me, "Lou, without a body of work and a gallery showing, I just don't feel I've earned the right to call myself an artist."

Michael Ray would not be surprised by Susan's comment. Ray is the creator of the Stanford Business School courses on creativity. He believes that creativity is within all of us and is essential for a great life. He also believes it is dominated by the "voice of judgment."

I've seen this up close. For years I worked with artists in a program codeveloped with my late colleague, Victoria Beckwith Graham, called The Artist's Voice. Artists were asked to stand and tell the group, "I am an artist. Let me tell you about my art—let me tell you about my inspiration." To a person they struggled to do it. When they did, there was a palpable confrontation with the impostor mindset or the voice of judgment.

Studies on the impostor mindset have zeroed in on graduate students, physicians, nurses, and professionals of all descriptions. In short, no one is out of its reach.

According to a recent survey by Advantage Hill Partners, the biggest fear among executives at the C-Suite level is being found to be incompetent. This fear damages their confidence and undermines relationships. The other most common fears are underachieving; appearing too vulnerable; being politically attacked by colleagues, which causes mistrust and overcaution; and appearing foolish, which limits the ability to speak up or have honest conversations.

> **"Very few people, whether you've been in that job before or not, get into the seat and believe today that they are now qualified to be the CEO. They're not going to tell you that, but it's true."**
>
> – HOWARD SCHULTZ,
> chair, president, and CEO of Starbucks

The Trigger Called Public Speaking

If you've ever spoken publicly, maybe you've had a moment of impostor thinking. You're called to the front of the room, and when you stand, for a second you think to yourself, "I have no idea what I could have done to qualify me to speak on this topic. They are going to see I don't know what I'm talking about!"

This is not your private boogeyman. It happens to everybody at some level, at one time or another, which is why Jerry Seinfeld's joke about public speaking endures: "Most of us would rather be in our casket than stand and give the eulogy at a funeral."

It is a funny line because it's true. Surveys actually suggest that among phobias, including the fear of death, public speaking is the number one fear. Why? The fear that we will fail to meet the standard, look bad in front of others, stumble in public, and be criticized as incompetent is our worst nightmare.

This is why public speaking is practically a universal

trigger for impostor thinking, as well as a laboratory for confronting it.

To be sure, it takes more than an exploration into public speaking to fight the impostor mindset. It takes real work to turn your focus from yourself to making an honest connection with others. But you can learn how by practicing "Authentic Speaking."

I should explain at this point that I've devoted my life and career to helping people find their original voices, which is the source of their influence and power. I've found that through deliberate practice of being present and speaking from the heart, people can visit that space more often and strengthen their voices, which are completely and utterly original.

Not You?

Now if this isn't you, if you don't have impostor thoughts, you may know or love someone who does. You can recognize them by the way they shun compliments.

People with the impostor mindset don't attribute their success to their own capabilities, so they squirm a bit when they're recognized. They're not just being modest. They're uncomfortable with taking credit. They deflect compliments by saying things like:

"You're too kind."

"I really didn't do that much."

"You're exaggerating."

"I was at the right time, right place."

"I got lucky."

"My teammates are the talented ones."

"I just had to work twice as hard as everyone else."

"It's not that big of a deal."

"Thanks—I'll send you a check later (ha-ha)."

Another "tell" is that you will hear of their awards and promotions from other people, not from them. People with the impostor mindset don't celebrate their achievements because they feel unearned.

> **"The exaggerated esteem in which my lifework is held makes me very ill at ease. I feel compelled to think of myself as an involuntary swindler."**
> – ALBERT EINSTEIN

We are also gluttons for professional punishment. We wind up in workplaces where there is so much competitive pressure to win that people don't talk about their failures. This is fertile ground for impostor thinking at any level.

I worked for big broadcasting companies for more than a decade. I loved the business, and I loved my teammates. But broadcasting is a monthly push-push-push for revenue and ratings. Every time I slam-dunked a project, I felt a little relief, but it was like cotton candy—a blast of sweet that dissolved too quickly. Once the initial phase of accomplishment was behind me, it no longer seemed real. Soon I began to worry about the next ratings report from Arbitron. I was a caught in a cycle.

THE ENDLESS CYCLE OF "FAKE" ACCOMPLISHMENT

Note: this is an adaptation and simplification of the impostor cycle (Clance 1985).

The Perfectionism Come-On

The impostor syndrome usually includes the game of perfectionism. If you not only do a project well, but also do it perfectly, you'll buy yourself some extra points. The accomplishment is a bit more satisfying. If it's not perfect, you lose major points. Worse, if you make mistakes along the way, those mistakes will steal away your inner focus and cancel the accomplishment all together.

In my corporate career, I fretted over every error and every detail left uncovered. I remember one night I got home after working late, and as I got into bed I realized I had left a minor typo in a memo I had distributed. This was before email. I couldn't sleep. So I got dressed, got back in my car at midnight, and drove back to the station to retype that memo. No one ever knew. Even a typo would hint at my incompetence.

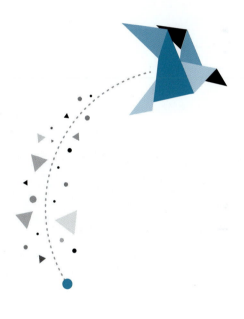

I consider my accomplishments inadequate for my stage in life.

I really didn't do that much.

People tend to believe I'm more talented than I really am.

I don't deserve

You're too kind

It's not that big of a deal.

My teammates are the talented ones.

perfectionism

fake

You're too kind.

I got lucky.

I was at the right time, right place.

the recognition

I consider my accomplishments inadequate for my stage in life.

People tend to believe I'm more talented than I really am.

Hiding

SECTION II

FREEING THE RADICAL HERO

Miracle Readiness

For me, breaking the code to the impostor mindset first requires a look into the four rooms of miracle-readiness. Any of us can look to these rooms when we've lost our rhythm in life. But the process is essential if you are preparing for and maintaining a shift in perception, which can be miraculous for the impact it can have on your life.

Reflection, prayer, meditation, and deep breathing for just a few minutes every day can help clear your mind of negative thinking and ward off the impostor mindset.

Human **Connections** are restorative. Build a strong and loving network of genuine people who want the best for you. Alex "Sandy" Pentland at Massachusetts Institute of Technology calls these folks "kithmates" who offer comfort, encouragement, and validation.

Wellness on a physical level requires that we stop putting toxic substances into our bodies and clear away the fog of any self-medication. Exercise, rest, and nutrition are critical too (a tough one for me since I love snacks).

Resilience and resolve of the heart and mind to take action can never be underestimated. Don't trip over your ego or the stigma of therapy or counseling if you can benefit from conversation with an expert. Insist on being happy. Otherwise, you'll have little to offer the world.

Confronting the Self-Talk

We all talk to ourselves in our thoughts, and research suggests that most of our thoughts are negative. For me, impostor thinking is like having a judgmental best friend in your head who constantly slips in critical comments about you. I've named mine. I call her Ms. Vader, after Darth Vader.

> "A sense of humor will help get a girl out of a dark place."
> — TWYLA THARP

Of course, the human psyche is more complicated than a sci-fi character. But the impostor syndrome withers when we make fun of it. Humor can also be a tool to avoid becoming heavy with self-introspection. I found that giving her a name helped me be deliberate in the practice of calling out impostor thoughts. Ms. Vader sounds like this:

"You don't belong here."

"Well, you got close, but you still screwed it up!"

"You don't deserve to be here with these people—they are really smart."

"You might have gotten by this time, but you'll never be able to pull it off again."

"Don't say anything about your award. It was just luck anyway."

"No way you're as talented as they think you are."

"You did okay, but it was nothing special."

Your Radical Hero

Once I began to notice the voice of Ms. Vader, I realized the one noticing was my radical hero.

radical hero: one who challenges the oppression of negative thinking and fights for freedom.

Call it intuition or divine intervention, my radical hero has a wiser view of life. She recognizes propaganda. When noticing a nasty comment from Ms. Vader, she asks, "Is that really true? Nah. Truth doesn't sound like that."

"The four questions are:
1) Is it true?
2) Can you absolutely know that it's true?
3) How do you react, what happens, when you believe that thought? and
4) Who would you be without the thought?"

– BYRON KATIE

I've named my radical hero too. I call her Bette Lou, which is the name given me by my beautiful Southern mother, Peggy. Growing up I was embarrassed by it. I thought it revealed something unsophisticated about me. Today I know Bette Lou is strong beyond measure.

I first heard my radical hero when I was about ten years old. I lay in my bed upstairs, above the shouting below. I heard the calm but certain voice say, "This is not who you are. You're going to be free." My radical hero was holding my resolve in safe keeping.

Impostor thinking does not win out 100 percent of the time. Even in the most difficult stretches, I experienced bursts of inspiration from my radical hero—a deep, essential knowing that I was meant for something greater.

We all need occasional help from our radical hero, don't we? Whether it is equating our worth to a tough college admission, comparing ourselves to the images of perfection in the media and becoming hyper self-conscious, or feeling bad if we don't crush every project at work, all human beings understand what it means to feel "not good enough." We need a message, a whisper, from the one who knows the truth.

> "When you have a dream, it doesn't come at you screaming in your face, 'This is who you are!' The hardest thing to listen to—your instincts, your human personal intuition—always whispers. Every day of your lives be ready to hear what whispers in your ear."
>
> —STEVEN SPIELBERG

Exercises Ahead

From this point forward in the book, there are prompts and exercises. We've given you lots of space to come back and respond to the prompts at another time. Your villain is likely to say, "This is lame." Do it anyway. Simply jot random thoughts as they come up. It is the process of writing and not the outcome that offers clarity.

> **What is your villain saying to you? Download. Write down the most ridiculous trash thoughts about yourself. You will never show these to anyone, but getting them from the inside to the outside drains their power.**

NOTES

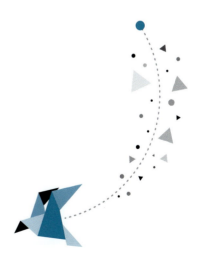

> **Cast this liar into a character, so you can listen for the voice and make fun of it. What's the name that comes to mind?**

NOTES

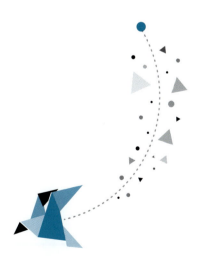

> **Describe the traits of the one who can see through the lies. Who is the one who knows the truth?**

NOTES

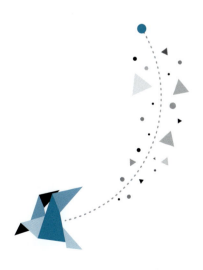

> **What would be a spirited name for your radical hero—something or someone you associate with being genuine and good?**

NOTES

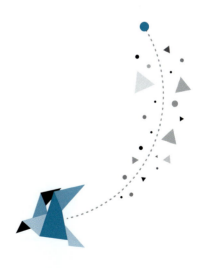

Resilience and resolve of the heart and mind
to take action can never be underestimated

Confronting the Self-Talk

Wellness
take action
resolve

Miracle

Reflection

Build a strong and
loving network

Connection

preparing for and maintaining
a shift in perception

Human Connections
are restorative

validation   **my inner voice**

challenge oppression and
fight for freedom

heart and mind

Readiness

Resilience

clear your mind of
negative thinking
and ward off the
impostor mindset.

Insist on being happy

encouragement

SECTION III

LIES AND LIMITING BELIEFS

My radical hero has helped me hack into at least five limiting beliefs that once kept me isolated. They have dissolved slowly and then quickly. It has taken deliberate practice, and I'm still practicing.

Limiting Belief #1
Control Is Power; Vulnerability Is Weakness

Growing up in a military home, the concept of "vulnerability" was like kryptonite. It meant weakness, deficiency in war, and exposure to imminent attack. My father taught me that the goal was to pull yourself up by your bootstraps and control your destiny. The house rule was to never ask for help and "never let them see you sweat." From my years as a teenager through my twenties, I strained to maintain control, to be cool—always in charge.

In my early thirties I had a bit of a breakdown. I hit a wall with mental, physical, and emotional exhaustion. I reached out to a friend I respected, Gregg. I told him, "I constantly feel as though I don't belong—that I don't deserve to be where I am." There. I said it out loud. I had taken the first and most vital step to freedom, which is recognition of the problem.

It was painfully awkward to be that vulnerable, to be

seen in the light of day. I had been fiercely independent for so long. But at the same time, I began to feel the relief and the empowerment that comes from letting go. I asked Gregg for help sorting it all out. We put together an action plan that would eventually lead me to Barbara.

People ask me, "How can vulnerability be empowering?" I tell them it's what the impostor voice fears most. Once you allow yourself to be seen, the voice has nowhere to go. It crumbles like a dirt clod.

Herein lies the great paradox: the seduction of acting invulnerable comes from an upside-down idea that it will keep you safe. Meanwhile, your vulnerability is where your humanity resides. It's where your unique contribution to the world has its roots. It's what people love about you. It is the ultimate freedom to be who you are.

A HUMAN MOMENT

Back during the recession of 2009, I was one of the many small business owners who struggled to stay in business. When asked how business was going, my stock answer was, "Oh, you know, slow but steady."

One morning I was leaving a business breakfast and ran into my friend Catharine, a real estate executive and a wonderful spitfire of a human being. When she asked about my business, instead of pretending everything was fine, I told her that I was worried that I didn't have what it took to be a small business owner in the recession.

Catharine stopped and grabbed my forearm. She looked me in the eye and said, "Punch it in the gut, Lou. We need you out here. Punch this thing in the gut."

As I drove out of the parking lot that morning, I passed Catharine walking to her car. She waived and threw a karate kick in the air. I belly laughed. I was lifted by not only her humor but also a moment of vulnerability and another hero who drew me forward.

We need authentic human encounters—the physical presence of another human being along with their complete attention—like oxygen. Reaching out even in a brief moment hacks away at isolation and fear.

"The human moment is an authentic psychological encounter that can only happen when two people share the same physical space and focus on one another. Together, you quickly create a force field of exceptional power. The positive effects of a human moment can last long after the people involved have said goodbye and walked away. People begin to think in new and creative ways; mental activity is stimulated."

– DR. EDWARD HALLOWELL

> **Invulnerability doesn't keep us safe. Trying to convince ourselves and others that everything is "fine" only keeps us in isolation. Write down the genuine concerns you ignore when you say everything is "fine."**

NOTES

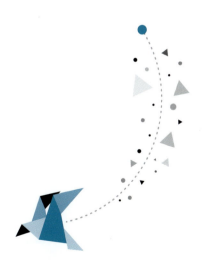

❯ **Can you recall a time when you let down your guard—for an authentic moment with another human being that seemed to give you life? What happened?**

NOTES

> **What holds you back from seeking out more of these moments? What is the risk?**

NOTES

> **What future can you envision if you keep a tight grip on invulnerability?**

NOTES

> **Who might you be without that grip?**

NOTES

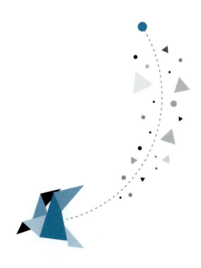

❯ **What is your best opportunity to experience a human moment this week?**

NOTES

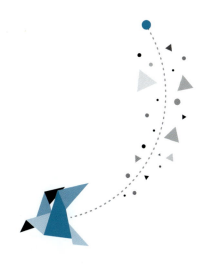

Limiting Belief #2
There's Nothing Original or Gifted about Me

I've found that people with the impostor mindset know very little about their natural strengths. Since we think we've only pretended to have talent, we're detached from our unique abilities.

Radical Hero Strengths Inventory

The Radical Hero Strengths Inventory is a simple email that you send to people you trust to give you feedback on what you do well. Here's an example:

> Dear Fran:
> I am doing some research into my strengths—for self-awareness, and as a means to leverage what I do well.
> It has been suggested that I reach out to the people who interact with me often enough to know my work and style of communication. Since you certainly fall into that category, I have a request.
> Please take a moment to jot a few thoughts

about my best abilities, what I'm good at, what you depend on me for. Go with your impulses, and don't worry about editing.

I would be grateful if you could reply within the week.

Thanks for helping me out,
[Your name]

Send your own version of the note to eight to ten people whose opinions you respect and who know you well. These people can be friends, family members, colleagues, classmates—anyone who has been in a position to see you demonstrate your abilities over time.

So often someone will say to me, "Don't I need to ask people for the negative feedback—that's the real stuff. They're going to say nice things about me because I'm putting them on the spot."

I had the same concern, but for this one exercise, I did it anyway. And the most amazing thing happened. When I looked at the results, consistent themes surfaced, and my strengths stepped out into view. It was a revelation to find that people close to me recognized the things that are so important to me—things like compassion and deep listening.

I can tell you that when we ask people to do this as a part of our courses, they are surprised to find that recipients are honored to be considered a resource, and they want to provide thoughtful feedback. It's meaningful to tell someone what you value about them, and we rarely have the format to do so.

There will be other times in life where it makes sense to look at what you're not so good at, but this is not where folks with the impostor syndrome need help. We need help learning about our authenticity and our gifts.

Don't shy away from this. It's extremely important material for you to use in stretching your perception.

Inventory Themes

Notice the common threads, themes, and patterns in the feedback. To have fooled everyone into thinking you are intelligent and talented in the same way, you would have to be a great magician, traveling with a smoke machine and trick mirrors.

Be with this feedback and own it. Allow yourself to accept what others appreciate about you—and take their word for it.

Jot down your thoughts about each theme. What resonates with you, and what surprises you?

Allow all the fragments to come together into a whole person who is known for the very strengths that are important to you.

❯ My Top Five Strengths

1.

2.

3.

4.

5.

NOTES

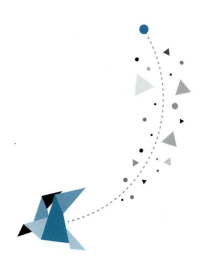

Limiting Belief #3
A Successful Career Is a Successful Life

I spent too many years believing that occupational success was *the* measure of intelligence and talent and that being productive was the only way to build self-worth. I rushed through college and earned my undergraduate degree by the age of twenty. I sprinted toward a great career that I thought would save me so that the universe would issue me a passport to happiness and belonging.

I landed in broadcast marketing and worked for a couple of iconic radio stations over the course of twelve years. I loved the business. I worked 24/7 and thought of nothing else.

But one night my friend Liz called and told me to turn on the local news quickly. A reporter on our sister television station was breaking the news that our station was being sold. In a shortsighted move that would later be regretted, my beloved parent company sold "my" radio station. The lack of information and disregard for the employees that followed made me realize the job would never take care of me. For me, the sale was like being served divorce papers.

Within a few weeks, the new general manager, George, came to meet with us and explain the acquisition and pending reorganization. Sitting in the conference room, I heard my radical hero whisper, "It's time to go." At the end of the meeting, I walked down the hall to my office, closed the door, and typed up my resignation. Within two weeks I was working for the NPR affiliate in town for half the money. My friends thought I was crazy.

At the NPR station, I fell in love with the power of storytelling. I had time to take a few night courses for the enjoyment of learning. I could see my life as a growing process instead of a string of achievements.

I used to think that pushing myself to the ragged edge helped me produce inspired work. But lowering the pressure actually allowed my originality and purpose to show up.

> "I will have a calling."
>
> – ANGELA DUCKWORTH

SPONTANEITY, HUMOR, AND PLAY

Perfectionism can rob us of being playful since we don't want to risk being seen as "silly." There was a point at which I had lost the ability to be spontaneous and joyfully present.

Today I practice the big medicine of humor and playfulness. When I'm with my Interact teammates, we erupt into laughter and good energy. At home I sing show tunes to my dogs. I do impersonations (pretty good ones, too) with friends and family. I found Erica, a wide-open radical hero who teaches dance fitness and helps people get back their groove.

I still have days when I take myself too seriously, but I have people in my life who can call me on it.

> **Which comes closest to your orientation to work:
1) a career built upon achievement that offers powerful titles, validation, and prestige; or
2) work as a form of self-expression and personal fulfillment? Or are you somewhere in between? Explain.**

NOTES

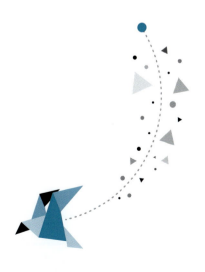

> **Regardless of your orientation, which elements of your work are the most meaningful?**

NOTES

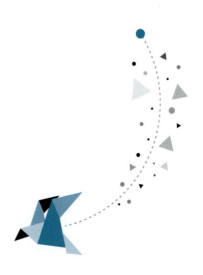

> **What do you instinctively know is missing in your work?**

NOTES

❯ If there were no constraints, what kind of work would you do (in your wildest dreams)?

NOTES

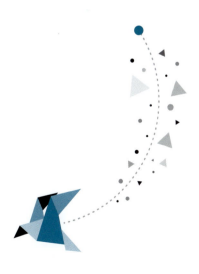

> **Name one step you can take this week to increase your personal expression at work—from developing a relationship to modifying an activity. Shake it up.**

NOTES

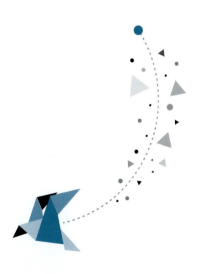

> "Owning our story can be hard but not nearly as difficult as spending our lives running from it."
>
> – BRENÉ BROWN

Limiting Belief #4
I Don't Have a Real Story

Growing up I was taught to "never air your dirty laundry." Isn't "dirty laundry" an awful name for your family life? I thought we should be embarrassed and hide family matters because they were dirty. I thought that if people knew, they would see me as flawed and use it against me.

So by the time I became a young adult, I had so much hidden that I felt anonymous. It became vital for me to uncover and own my story. I found I could not only make sense of the past, but also build a better future in the process.

Future Building

Storytelling has a way of celebrating the beauty and messiness of life while making sense of it for a bigger, better future. By putting my experience into words, the universe had powerful purpose and organization.

> **"When we translate an experience into language, we essentially make the experience graspable."**
>
> – DR. JAMES PENNEBAKER

There is a four-phase process of harvesting your story:
- **I.** Early Influences
- **II.** Recent Influences
- **III.** Connecting the Dots
- **IV.** Journey of the Radical Hero

What follows is a series of prompts to help you uncover your story.

> "I write because I don't know what I think until I read what I say."
>
> - FLANNERY O'CONNOR

❯ I. Early Influences

There are a few basic areas to inventory that will help uncover your "backstory" or early influences to retrieve a sense of self. Respond to the ones that hold the most power.

- Geography
- Family
- Parent Talents
- Radical Heroes and Role Models
- Early Interests

NOTES

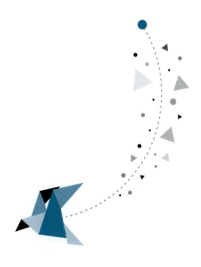

● Geography

Where were you raised? Describe the traits, the geography, or the history of your hometown.

How did it influence you? If you moved a good bit, describe what that was like. What did you learn?

NOTES

● Family

How many siblings do you have, and where do you fall in the birth order?

What was that like?
What did you learn?

NOTES

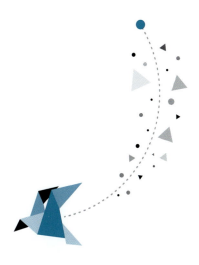

● Parent Talents

What were the talents or career choices of your parents?

What did they want for you? How are you like or unlike them?

NOTES

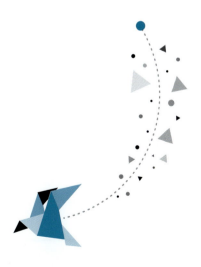

● Radical Heroes and Role Models

Teachers, coaches, and relatives can have impact on our lives. Name the individuals who had a positive influence on you. What did you learn from them?

* Negative role models can demonstrate the opposite way you want to live.

NOTES

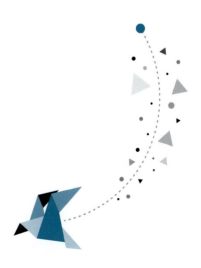

● Early Interests

What were your early studies and activities—subjects, sports, or hobbies in or outside of school?

What about these activities did you love? What were the wins, losses or disappointments?

NOTES

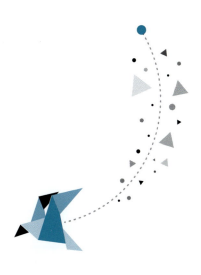

II. Recent Influences

Here are areas to inventory that will help uncover your recent influences. Respond to the ones that are most relevant to you.

- Education
- Jobs, Breaks, and Big Projects
- Relationships
- Radical Heroes and Role Models
- Travels

NOTES

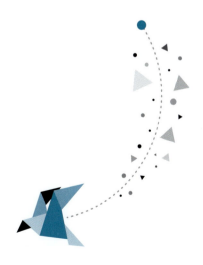

● Education

What experiences in education—choice of studies, friends, teachers, and professors—had an impact on you?

NOTES

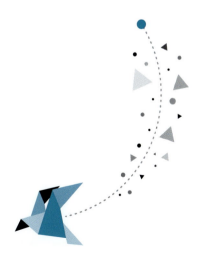

● Jobs, Breaks, and Big Projects

What jobs and projects have been especially meaningful? What have you learned?

NOTES

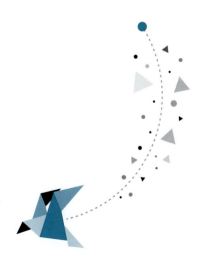

● Relationships

Name the most significant events related to your personal relationships—chance meetings, proposals, weddings, and births.

NOTES

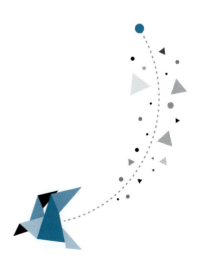

● Radical heroes and Role Models

Name the individuals who had an important influence on you. What did you learn?

NOTES

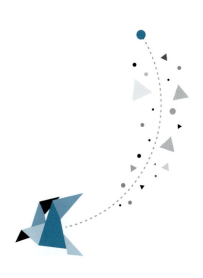

● **Travels**

What travels and adventures have made a mark on you?

NOTES

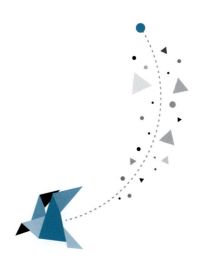

▶ III. Connecting the Dots

By now, you should have four to six influences that have shaped you. These people, places, and events might be about love, inspiration, winning, loss, or defeat. What's important is that you begin to see them as your collective wisdom. They represent an opportunity to share with others what your life has taught you.

Write a simple short story that connects these influences.

NOTES

NOTES

NOTES

▶ IV. The Radical Hero's Journey

Beloved author Joseph Campbell taught us that the hero's journey is an ancient story embedded in the human experience. It has been present across every culture since the beginning of time. The hero is you, me, and everyone in our human experience.

The present-day hero's journey goes something like this: You are living life as usual when something happens to call you to a journey of change. The call can be the loss of something precious, hitting bottom with something that's not working, or a deep feeling of dissatisfaction.

As you head into the unknown, things are no longer "steady as she goes." Change is difficult, and you are tested. Along the way you find mentors and other heroes who offer encouragement and validation.

In a crucial moment of the journey, you make the decision to stand up to the challenge and move through it.

As you overcome the hardship, you gain a greater understanding of life. You are stronger than you know. You are rewarded with wisdom to empower others and return home with much more than you had when you left.

Journeys range from a day or a week to the course

JOURNEY OF THE RADICAL HERO

of a lifetime, and everything in between. They offer obstacles great and small, each with the opportunity to gain wisdom and empower others.

What follows is a series of prompts that will help you reflect on your own journey.

> **Think of the events that have disrupted "life as usual" for you. Name and describe them.**

NOTES

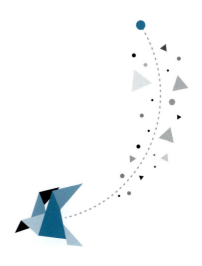

> **Leaving that which is familiar after a disruption and stepping into the unknown can be frightening. Describe what you experienced.**

NOTES

❯ Was there a specific mentor who helped with a disruption—someone who encouraged you to keep going? Name and describe the individual. Even a stranger can offer words of encouragement.

NOTES

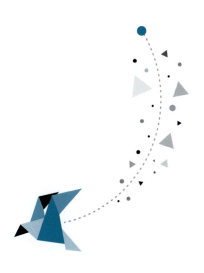

❯ **Think of a time when you found the courage you needed to move through a challenge. Describe what happened.**

NOTES

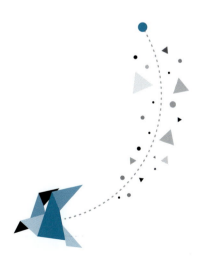

> **How have you surprised yourself when overcoming adversity?**

NOTES

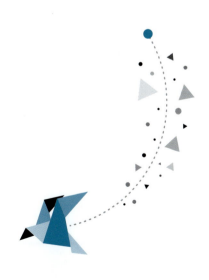

> **Once you realize you're on the other side of an ordeal, you are not the same. You have gained the wisdom that can help others. Describe the learning you share with others. How has it shaped your life?**

NOTES

❯ From Step IV, summarize your radical hero's journey as you now understand it. You will have many journeys. Write about the one that has the most heat.

NOTES

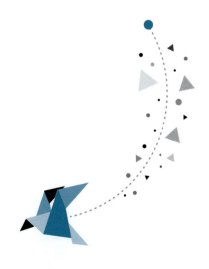

NOTES

NOTES

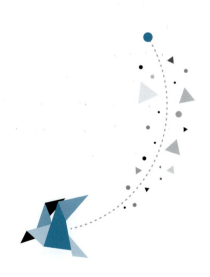

This is a good start. You now have an overview of your influences and a snapshot of one of your journeys. As you begin this work, there will be a deepening of your understanding. More defining events will occur to you. The radical hero's journey never ends. You will face another call to shake things up. There is always another adventure ahead.

People ask me, "Lou, isn't it dangerous to overshare in inappropriate situations?" Of course it is. Common sense has to prevail about the where and the when. But when it's time—you'll know it. And despite moments of doubt, you must believe there is power in your story. Knowing it and using bits and pieces in your communication will keep you from trying to convince anyone of who you are. Threads of wisdom that require vulnerability will make our lives richer.

The story of your life is the value that comes from your experience. To share with others what your life has taught you (to empower them) is the essence of generosity.

"Becoming present is not just about knowing and affirming your story—it's also about how you narrate your story. Telling yourself what matters to you is one thing, but equally important is taking control of how you tell your story—to yourself and to others."

– AMY CUDDY

DELIBERATE PRACTICE

Not long ago I worked with Andrew, an attorney who is highly respected and accomplished in his practice. He is also charming and kind. Andrew called me one day and said, "I just have to do something. I've hit bottom." He explained that for years he had turned down invitations to speak on his best advice on being successful in a field that has become crowded and competitive.

Most recently Andrew had passed on an invitation from a colleague to speak to a group of attorneys at a prestigious event, giving the excuse he would be out of town that week. As luck would have it, he saw his friend in the produce section of the grocery store one night and had to dodge him.

"I felt like a fool," Andrew said. "Here I was a grown man, at the height of my career, hiding behind the bananas."

We had a good laugh and talked about the irrational voice that comes with impostor thinking.

Andrew is not alone. I have worked with scores of accomplished people, including architects, physicians, rabbis, bankers, accountants, ministers, and musicians. They all say the same thing, in so many words: "I don't have an interesting story. I'm afraid they'll find out I don't know what I'm talking about."

Andrew began the process of deliberate practice of authentic speaking. He came to my studio and told his stories. He spoke from the heart and learned to visit this space more often. We videotaped those stories and watched them together. He practiced using his life lessons in messages. We identified goals. He practiced physical confidence. He would go away and reflect on the process and tell me about his experience when he returned. He began to accept invitations to speak. In time he gained the confidence to turn his focus from himself to others.

> **"Whether it means to learn to dance by practicing dancing or to learn to live by practicing living, the principles are the same."**
> – MARTHA GRAHAM

Don't miss what so-called public speaking can do for you–if you practice going beyond technique into authenticity. It allows you to struggle and repetition allows you to release the struggle. It's a wonderful test kitchen of becoming more and more of who you really are.

Limiting Belief #5
Loud Talkers Are in Charge

For the first ten years of my life, I had a very small voice. My words got stuck in my throat and took my breath away. In the presence of criticism, I couldn't speak at all. Ultimately I believed that loud talkers were in charge. Shouting was a weapon.

But in high school, a radical hero named Coach Tavenier planted a precious seed within me. Coach was my biology teacher. With a twinkle in his eye, he would say, "I'm listening for brilliance, people!" He delighted in listening to our ideas. He taught us that brilliance was not about knowing the answers; it was giving voice to our imagination.

> **"Listening is a magnetic and strange thing, a creative force. When we really listen to people there is an alternating current, and this recharges us so that we never get tired of each other. We are constantly being re-created."**
>
> – BRENDA UELAND

One day I raised my hand and asked a question. Coach listened thoughtfully and said with broad smile, "Bette Lou, you've got a wonderful mind for science!" He was completely present and I felt those words. I have never forgotten Coach Tavenier or the idea of listening for brilliance—of drawing people forward with the generosity of your attention and belief in them.

Perhaps you've noticed that when you're with someone who listens to you deeply and believes in you, you feel at home, original, and interesting.

It isn't so difficult to be like Coach Tavenier. With our friends, kids, students, and family, we can notice their talent and say, "Wow, you're really good at this," or "You have a gift around this." The impostor mindset is snuffed out in the light of sincere attention.

What's at stake if we don't empower brilliance? We'll never tap into the best ideas among people who might just solve the world's problems—that's for certain. If left unchecked, the impostor voice can lead to isolation, anxiety, burn out, depression, stalled projects, and unfinished masterpieces, not to mention dissatisfaction and an unhappy life.

Strong and Silent

A friend named Emily told me a story about her dad, John, and a ride the two of them took in his old Corvette many years ago. John was a "strong and silent" man who had worked with his hands his entire life. He was generous when people needed help. He listened deeply to the world around him. In his spare time, he loved being in the garage, working on that old car.

After law school, Emily had built a successful law practice and was running her own firm, but she was unhappy. She felt the pull to walk away from the practice and teach law instead. Her colleagues were shocked, and Emily was worried that her father would be too. He had invested so much to send her to law school. He was so proud of her.

Emily tried to begin the conversation with him several times, but couldn't bring herself to say the words. One day she called him and said, "I need to talk to you, Dad." He paused for a moment and said, "Why don't you come by and we'll take a ride in the Corvette?"

She went to see him that day, and they took a ride. That's what they did when they needed to talk. Side by side they watched the road ahead until she broke the silence and told him about her dream. Mustering a bit of courage, Emily said, "I know how much you've invested, Dad. I'm worried about disappointing you. But I'm wrestling with the idea of leaving my practice."

After a pause her Dad replied, "I would be disappointed if you didn't." A few words in that old Corvette in a moment of deep listening have become one of the links in Emily's life that gives it meaning.

WHAT PEOPLE SAY ABOUT NOT BEING HEARD

In today's environment, it's easy to travel in our own self-enclosed orbits, focused on our agendas. In our workshops at Interact Studio, we invite people to pair up and participate in an exercise that demonstrates how communicators "run out of gas" when their listeners suddenly look away, disengage, and pull out their smart phones. When we ask the speaker how it felt when their listeners looked away, the responses include: "I felt discounted;" "I was unable to continue;" "I lost my train of thought;" "I started rambling;" and "I forgot what I was going to say."

Can you go through a whole day listening deeply to everyone around you? No. But you can notice when your teammates, friends, and family need your complete attention. Watch for the opportunity to listen in a way that releases people into full expression.

> **Think of a powerful conversation that has stayed with you forever. What happened, and how has it shaped you?**

NOTES

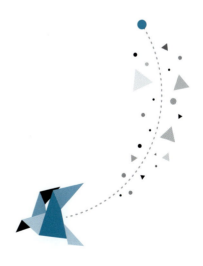

❯ When was the last time someone listened to you deeply? What happened?

NOTES

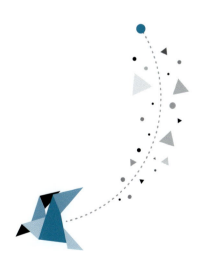

> **What is the situation or story within you that needs to come out with the help of someone who listens deeply?**

NOTES

> **When was the last time you listened to someone deeply? What happened?**

NOTES

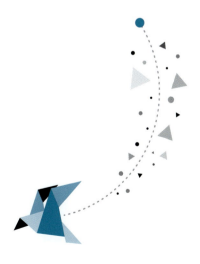

> **Consider the people in your immediate circle of friends, family, and teammates. Who might need your listening at the moment?**

NOTES

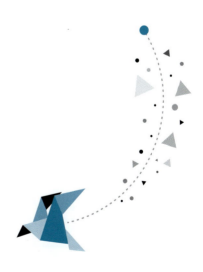

The Way It Is Today

I have never "arrived." There have been stagnant spots when I just did the leg-work—and I practiced. Calling out impostor thoughts is a lifetime assignment. Over time, inner peace comes for longer stretches.

Today, when Ms. Vader shows up and hurls an insult, she has no mask. I know what's happening most of the time. My radical hero has gotten louder and says, "Ha! That was rich."

I have also found that at some level, most of us feel as though we're on the outside looking in. For years I've seen it on the faces of people in my classes. As I describe the impostor mindset, there is a trace of the dawning I felt when I first heard the term from Barbara. The very word "impostor" seems to capture their sense of not belonging to this world—of occasionally feeling like a "troubled guest."

Today my life is one story, loaded with beautiful brokenness, vulnerability, redemption, purpose, and joy. It all works together.

I've gained such optimism about the human spirit. I have found that when people stand and tell their stories and allow themselves to be vulnerable, we are in the presence of greatness. The gray status quo clears, and we are connected in color. We are less fearful. We are more trusting, and we are trusted. We are no longer impostors. We are radical heroes.

    Never settle for less.

"Rather than speak from the false self, there is a more radical, silent self, which is the outlaw view of creation. To be yourself and put that self into conversation with others, to hear yourself say things you did not know you knew—this is your identity and poetic imagination."

– David Whyte

SUPPLEMENT

Ten Tools for Overcoming the Impostor Mindset

1 Name it and take the power out of it. Find the friend to whom you can say, "Sometimes I feel like a fraud." Being able to say that out loud to another person can lighten the burden immediately. You might be surprised to hear how much your friend understands and needed to hear it from you.

2 Argue your case. With the help of a friend, make a factual list of your accomplishments. Try to convince your friend you had no role in these successes. Just try.

3 Practice generosity. A mind turned inward is a painful thing. The fastest way to get over feeling like a fake is to turn your thoughts toward someone you can help. Look around you. Who could use a connection?

4 Learn something. Studies show that learning creates a healthy self-image. Gaining new insights has a way of pushing out old ones. Take a class, do some research, or pick up a hobby you've always longed to try.

5 Do some spring cleaning. Not long ago, I was sitting at my desk and felt something lurking. I realized I had been hanging framed certificates of accomplishment on the wall behind me for so long that I could feel them breathing down my neck. So I took them all down and had the wall painted. I don't need them anymore.

6 Lighten up. It's boring to take yourself so seriously. If you have a giggle buddy who can help you let go of some of that heaviness and laugh at yourself, you will feel less like a fake. Make a conscious effort to include humor, fun, and spontaneity in your life.

7 Collect your thank-you notes, cards, and emails. Go through them when you're feeling like a fraud. All of these people have not conspired to give you fake comments.

8 Embrace imperfection. Whenever you can, admit that you don't know everything and ask others what they think. People will recognize you as genuine and trustworthy. The truth is that nobody knows exactly what's going on, and we all feel as though we're on the outside of things on a regular basis.

9 Do it for the ones you love. When you live life feeling that you don't deserve to be here, you can't possibly be there for people who need you. You are only a shell of the role model you were meant to be, and you are robbing us of the sacred contribution we can only get from you.

10 **Move forward.** Whatever you do, do something today, in spite of your doubts. The impostor mindset lives in intellection. It can't breathe when you take action. When you move forward, it gives us the permission to move forward as well. Open the door for us, and we'll be right behind you.

RESOURCES

Brown, B. 2012. *Daring Greatly: How the Courage to Be Vulnerable Transforms the Way We Live, Love, Parent, and Lead.* New York: Gotham.

Campbell, J. 2008. *The Hero with a Thousand Faces.* Novato, CA: New World Library.

Chrisman, S. M., W. A. Pieper, P. R. Clance, and C. L. Holland. 1995. "Validation of the Clance Impostor Phenomenon Scale." *Journal of Personality Assessment* 65(3): 456-467.

Clance, P. R. 1985. *The impostor phenomenon: Overcoming the fear that haunts your success.* Atlanta, Ga.: Peachtree Publishers.

Clance, P. R. 1985. *The Impostor Phenomenon: When Success Makes You Feel Like a Fake.* New York, NY: Bantam.

Clance, P. R., and S. A. Imes. 1978. "The Impostor Phenomenon in High Achieving Women: Dynamics and Therapeutic Intervention." *Psychotherapy: Theory, Research & Practice* 15(3): 241-247.

Cuddy, A. 2015. Presence: Bringing Your Boldest Self to Your Biggest Challenges. New York, NY: Little, Brown and Company.

Dweck, C. S. 2006. *Mindset: The New Psychology of Success.* New York, NY, US: Random House.

Fey, Tina. 2010. "From Spoofer to Movie Stardom." *The Independent* (March 19, 2010): http://www.independent.co.uk/arts-entertainment/films/features/tina-fey-from-spoofer-to-movie-stardom-1923552.html.

Galinsky, E., K. Salmond, J. T. Bond, M. B. Kropf, M. Moore, and M. Harrington, M. 2003. *Leaders in a Global Economy: A Study of Executive Women and Men*. New York: Catalyst. http://www.catalyst.org/knowledge/leaders-global-economy-study-executive-women-and-men.

Goleman, D. 2006. *Social Intelligence: The New Science of Human Relationships*. Random House: NY.

Gravois, J. 2007. "You're Not Fooling Anyone." *Chronicle of Higher Education*, 54 (11).

Harvey, J. C., and C. Katz. 1985. *If I'm Successful, Why Do I Feel Like a Fake?* New York, NY: St. Martin's Press.

Hallowell, E. 1999. "The Human Moment at Work." *Harvard Business Review*. January-February.

Holmes, S. W., L. Kertay, L. B. Adamson, and C. L. Holland, C. L. 1993. "Measuring the Impostor Phenomenon: A Comparison of Clance's IP Scale and Harvey's I-P Scale." *Journal of Personality Assessment* 60 (1): 48-59.

Jarrett, C. 2010. "Feeling Like a Fraud." *Psychologist* 23 (5): 380-383.

Kaplan, K. 2009. "Unmasking the Impostor." *Nature* 459 (7245): 468-469.

Katie, B., and S. Mitchell. 2003. *Loving What Is: Four Questions That Can Change Your Life*. New York: Penguin Random House.

RESOURCES

Langford, J., and P.R. Clance. 1993. "The Imposter Phenomenon: Recent Research Findings Regarding Dynamics, Personality and Family Patterns." *Psychotherapy: Theory, Research, Practice, Training* 30 (3): 495-501.

McGregor, L. N., D. E. Gee, and K. E. Posey. 2008. "I Feel Like a Fraud and It Depresses Me: The Relation Between the Imposter Phenomenon and Depression." *Social Behavior and Personality* 36(1): 43-48.

Mount, P., and S. Tardanico. 2014. *Beating the Impostor Syndrome*. Greensboro, NC: Center for Creative Leadership.

Murray B. 2002. "Writing to Heal: By Helping People Manage and Learn From Negative Experiences, Writing Strengthens Their Immune Systems as Well as Their Minds." *The American Psychological Association* 33 (6): 54.

Robinson, B. 2007. *Chained to the Desk: A Guidebook for Workaholics*. New York, New York: University Press.

Robinson, S. L., and S. K. Goodpaster. 1991. "The Effects of Parental Alcoholism on Perception of Control and Imposter Phenomenon." *Current Psychology: Research & Reviews* 10(1): 113-119.

Sandberg, S. 2013. *Lean In: Women, Work, and the Will to Lead*. New York: Random House.

Selby, C. L. B., and M. J. Mahoney. 2002. "Psychological and Physiological Correlates of Self-Complexity and Authenticity." *Constructivism in the Human Sciences* 7(1): 39-52.

Sittenfeld, C. 2000. "The Most Creative Man in Silicon Valley." *Fast Company Magazine*. https://www.fastcompany.com/40613/most-creative-man-silicon-valley

Tharp, T. 2003. *The Creative Habit: Learn It and Use It for Life*. New York: Simon & Schuster.

Topping, M. E., and E. B. Kimmel. 1985. "The Imposter Phenomenon: Feeling Phony." *Academic Psychology Bulletin* 7(2): 213-226.

Wrzesniewski, A., C. R. McCauley, P. Rozin & B. Schwartz, B. 1997. "Jobs, Careers, and Callings: People's Relations to Their Work." *Journal of Research in Personality*, 31, 21-33.

Whyte, D. 2010. *What to Remember When Waking: The Disciplines of an Everyday Life*. Louisville, CO: Sounds True Incorporated.

Young, V. 2004. *How to Feel as Bright and Capable as Everyone Seems to Think You Are: A Handbook for Women (and Men) Who Doubt Their Competence—But Shouldn't*. Northampton, MA.

Young, V. 2011. *The Secret Thoughts of Successful Women: Why Capable People Suffer from the Impostor Syndrome and How to Thrive in Spite of It*. New York: Crown Business

Acknowledgments: A Grateful Heart

To my Interact family of lion-hearts, Julie Haldane, Patrick Sheehan, Michael Rogers, Amber Lineback, Tina Tyler, Jackson Sveen, and Andy Ciordia.

To my book team at SPARK Publications, Fabi Preslar, Larry Preslar, Genna Baugh, Jim Denk, Sofi Preslar, and Melisa Graham.

Acknowledgment to the researchers who first gave us the language to explore the impostor mindset, psychologists Pauline Clance and Suzanne Imes.

To the authors, artists, and radical heroes whose light along the path has given me inspiration and strength:

Isabelle Allende	Edward Hallowell
Maya Angelou	Byron Katie
Brené Brown	Anne Lamott
Susan Cain	Robert McKee
Joseph Campbell	Henri Nouwen
Julia Cameron	Alex "Sandy" Pentland
Amy Cuddy	Pete Senge
Angela Duckworth	Steven Spielberg
Albert Einstein	Twyla Tharp
Ralph Waldo Emerson	Brenda Ueland
Tina Fey	David Whyte
Seth Godin	Marianne Williamson
Daniel Goleman	Bill G. Wilson

About the Author

Lou Solomon, MSOD, is the CEO and founder of Interact, a communications firm located in Charlotte, North Carolina. Her experience with the impostor mindset has been a gift since she developed the "Your Authentic Speaking Style" curriculum to help people find their voices. Her TEDx talk, "The Surprising Solution to the Impostor Syndrome," can be viewed on YouTube.

She is a member of the adjunct faculty at the McColl School of Business at Queens University. In 2012, Lou cofounded TWIST, the school's unique Conference for Women in Leadership, held each spring in Charlotte, North Carolina.

Lou lives in Charlotte with her husband, Sandy, and her three office mates, Jake, Charlie, and Odie.

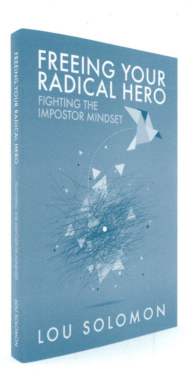

To explore a learning experience with Lou and the Interact Team at Interact Studio, please contact us at:

Interact Authentic Communication
Interact Studio 210
1435 West Morehead Street, Suite 210
Charlotte, NC 28208
interactauthentically.com
704.374.0423

🐦 InteractStudio

📘 Interact Authentic Communication

🌐 interactauthentically.com